DRAW ME

A TRIANGLE

BY ROBYN SUPRANER
PICTURES BY EVELYN KELBISH

NUTMEG PRESS

SIMON AND SCHUSTER

Copyright © 1970, Robyn Supraner
Copyright under the International Copyright Union

Published by Simon and Schuster, Children's Book Division
Rockefeller Center, 630 Fifth Avenue
New York, New York 10020

First printing

SBN 671-65155-2
Library of Congress Catalog Card Number: 78-124386
Manufactured in Italy

For my mother and father
with love

DRAW ME A TRIANGLE.
DRAW A DESIGN
WITH THREE CORNERS, A LINE
AND A LINE AND A LINE.
TRIANGLES ARE SHAPES
THAT ARE EASY TO FIND,
IF YOU OPEN YOUR EYES
AND YOU OPEN YOUR MIND.

BRIGHT YELLOW ROAD SIGNS,
ISLANDS, LIKE WEDGES,
AND BRIDGES ALL LACED UP
WITH NEAT, POINTED EDGES.

TRIANGLES DANCE
IN THE SWEET SUMMER BREEZE
AND THE KITES IN THE SKY
SING A SONG TO THE TREES.

WHILE OUT ON THE WATER,
SAILBOATS HAVE A RACE...
PENNANTS AND BANNERS
ALL OVER THE PLACE!

TODAY, LET US HAVE
A "TRIANGULAR TEA"...
APPLE TURNOVERS
FOR LAUREN AND ME.
DATE AND NUT SANDWICHES,
BLACKBERRY PIE,
AND CRISP LINEN NAPKINS
THAT POINT TO THE SKY!

SUMMERTIME TRIANGLES...
BUTTERFLY WINGS,
MOTHS ON A GRAPEVINE
GOSSAMER THINGS!
GAY PURPLE PANSIES,
SWEET CLOVER LEAVES,
HAYSTACKS IN THE MEADOW,
THE BARN'S HEAVY EAVES,
THE PEAKED ATTIC DORMER,
MY ARMS AS I LAY
IN THE GREEN FIELDS OF SUMMER,
ENJOYING THE DAY!

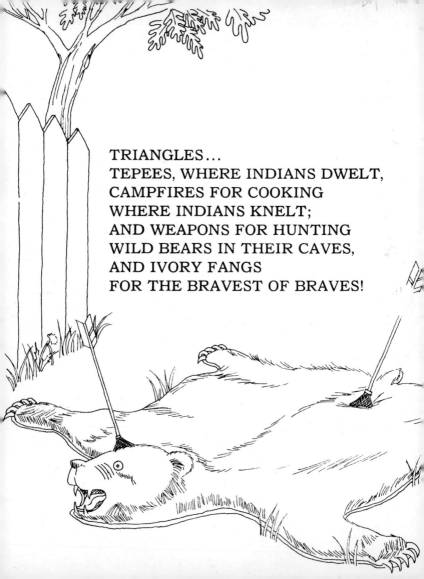

TRIANGLES...
TEPEES, WHERE INDIANS DWELT,
CAMPFIRES FOR COOKING
WHERE INDIANS KNELT;
AND WEAPONS FOR HUNTING
WILD BEARS IN THEIR CAVES,
AND IVORY FANGS
FOR THE BRAVEST OF BRAVES!

TRIANGLES ARE SWEET
LIKE A RASPBERRY ICE,
AND GLOBS OF WHIPPED CREAM,
AND MERINGUES, WHICH ARE NICE,
AND CHOCOLATE CUSTARD,
AND CHOCOLATE CAKE,
AND CHOCOLATE COOKIES
THAT PIERRE LOVES TO BAKE!

MAGICIANS AND CLOWNS
AND DUNCES PARADE
IN THE CRAZIEST HATS,
IN A GRAND PROMENADE!

THE TWINKLING STARS
SHINE LIKE SILVERY SPANGLES,
AND HALLOWEEN NIGHT
IS FILLED WITH TRIANGLES:
IN FAT JACK-O-LANTERNS,
DELECTABLE TREATS
LIKE CHOCOLATE KISSES
AND CANDY CORN SWEETS,
IN CACKLING WITCHES
WITH BLACK POINTY HATS,
AND GHOSTS IN THE MOONLIGHT,
AND VAMPIRE BATS!

A LETTER FROM MOZAMBIQUE,
FAR, FAR, AWAY,
ARRIVED WITH A MARVELOUS STAMP
JUST TODAY,
AND I THOUGHT HOW EXCITING
TO TRAVEL SO FAR,
DRESSED UP IN A STAMP
THAT IS TRI-ANG-U-LAR!

OUT OF TOWN

IN TOWN

GAY CHRISTMAS PRESENTS...
A FAN FROM AUNT ROSE,
AND NEAT LITTLE HANKIES
FOR AUNT MARTHA'S NOSE.
BRIGHT SILVER BELLS
ON A GREEN CHRISTMAS WREATH,
AND RED SATIN BOWS
AND WHITE DRAGON TEETH!
A PLAID WOOLEN SHAWL
TO WARM DEAR COUSIN BEA,
AND A BEAUTIFUL, SUGARPLUM,
CHRISTMASTIME TREE!

TRIANGLES...

SAYING YOUR PRAYERS
AT THE SIDE OF YOUR BED,
A BALLET POSITION,
A RATTLESNAKE'S HEAD,

A HANGER, A GOATEE,
THE POINT OF A SPEAR,
A DUCKLING'S WEBBED FOOT,
A PUSSYCAT'S EAR...

ON LAND AND ON SEA,
IN THE AIR...ALL AROUND,
ARE PLACES WHERE TRIANGLES
WAIT TO BE FOUND.

DRAW ME A TRIANGLE.
DRAW A DESIGN
WITH THREE CORNERS, A LINE
AND A LINE AND A LINE.